Animal Stories 2
For Families

Claire Suminski ♡

Susan Swedlund

Collected by
Claire Suminski
Illustrated by
Susan Swedlund
and Friends

First Edition
ISBN 978-1-7333559-8-8

Library of Congress Control Number: 2020947951

Published by Red Press Co.

Redpressco.com

Table of Tales

What time I am afraid, I will trust in thee.

When trouble, hard times, sickness, uncertainty , and more rain down upon us, it is tempting to be afraid. But God is bigger than all of our fears! Here are some encouraging words to remember from the Word of God.

Isaiah 35:4a
Say to them that are of a fearful heart, Be strong, fear not:

Psalm 34:4
I sought the LORD, and he heard me, and delivered me from all my fears.

Psalm 56:3-4
What time I am afraid, I will trust in thee.
In God I will praise his word, in God I have put my trust; I will not fear what flesh can do unto me.

Fear thou not for I am with thee: be not dismayed; for I am thy GOD.

II Timothy 1:7
For God hath not given us the spirit of fear; but of power, and of love, and of a sound mind.

I John 4:18 a
There is no fear in love; but perfect love casteth out fear:

Isaiah 41:10
Fear thou not; for I am with thee: be not dismayed; for I am thy God: I will strengthen thee; yea, I will help thee; yea, I will uphold thee with the right hand of my righteousness.

The Hungry Sea Lion

By Mike Kurczewski

This story is about a case of mistaken identity under the sea.

For a period of time, I worked as a trainer for PADI College, which is a scuba diving instructor training institution, located in Orange County, California. I was a course director, responsible for teaching scuba diving instructors. At one point we were doing advanced training for a group of instructor candidates from all over the United States and around the world. I met some very unique and talented individuals during that training.

We were staying at the USC Wrigley Marine Science Center on Catalina Island. You would think that after spending so much class time in the water, I would want to do something else on our night off, but that was not the case. I love to scuba dive!

It was well known by the locals that there were a lot of lobsters in nearby Fisherman's Cove. It seemed like it might make an interesting location for a night dive. The lobster grow very large in Fisherman's Cove because it is a protected area. The marine science center regularly studies marine life in this cove. There was a rock shelf tucked along the shore, known for its abundance of lobster.   One of my fellow staff members decided to go on this adventure with me and so we loaded up our gear and headed out from the boat dock. We were hoping to coax some of the larger lobster out from under the rock shelf for an under-water photo shoot.

I got there first and so busied myself, using the light on my camera to locate the lobster. I knew that my buddy would be joining me soon. Then all of a sudden, I felt him bump my shoulder. BUMP! That was a little annoying, but a few seconds later I felt a much harder bump on my back. BUMP-BUMP!   I started to turn around to give my buddy a little sign language lesson in dive courtesy, when all of a sudden, my whole body went on high alert! This was not my buddy, but a very big California Sea Lion pressing up against me!!!   He was apparently concerned that I was about to take his dinner!

Fast as I could, I swam out of the way, my heart beating fast. My buddy missed the whole thing. However, I managed to get a picture of the Sea Lion's backside trying to get the lobster out of the rocks. Proof that I really did have a close encounter of the Sea Lion kind!

The Short Stubborn Life of Hen-Rietta

by Marilyn Miller

My name is Marilyn and my husband, Don, and I live in a retirement park in Franklin, North Carolina. Right outside of our kitchen window is a thick hemlock tree where birds of all kinds take shelter before hopping onto the feeder nearby.

It has been a great source of pleasure for us to look into the tree as we stand at the sink and wash dishes. Can you imagine the surprise in my voice the day I looked out and said, "Hey, Hon? There's a hawk or turkey or something in the tree out there. Would you go out and see what it is, please?" He announced a few minutes later, "It's a CHICKEN!" We both burst out laughing since chickens are not native to our little community. In fact, in all the years we've lived here, we've never seen nor heard one anywhere around our place. So, WHERE did it come from? WHY was it in our tree? And more importantly, WHEN was it leaving? We have rules and restrictions in our park that state firmly, "No outdoor pets! Domesticated pets, indoors only."

This chicken was breaking the rules!

How to get a chicken to leave...let me count the ways... Picture if you will, two senior citizens circling a chicken in a tree and calling out, "SHOO!" But that chicken just ruffled her feathers and stared us down. We then tried shaking the branches gently, so as not to scare her to death, but she just flew to a higher branch. Finally, we shook the branches violently and hollered "SHOO! Get out of here!" as though we really meant it this time. She flew even higher up and stared down at us, rather boldly, I thought. She had taken up residence in our tree and was not about to leave! She even tried to make a nest in the pine straw around the base of the tree.

It was my sister who named our visitor Hen-Rietta, and she delighted in calling me on the phone to ask how Hen-Rietta and we were getting along.

Don and I were a bit put out by the stubborn refusal of this chicken to leave our premises. We had done everything, short of calling Animal Control. We decided to try stalking this single brown hen and throwing an old sheet over her. If we could get close enough to catch her, that is!

WHOOSH!!! Up she went into the air over our heads and she flew...she soared...like an eagle up to a tree on the hill next door. Well, yes. I know she's a bird too, but I didn't know that chickens could fly like THAT!   Why we didn't just leave her there, I can't say, but we foolishly pursued her with our outstretched sheets and again, she flew out of that tree, over our heads, landing on our roof down below. By the time we got back down the hill, she was once again comfortably established on her favorite branch in the hemlock tree.

"Hen-Rietta" made her home in our hemlock tree. We never fed her, but I think she ate the husks of the sunflower seeds that fell from the feeder. Perhaps she got water from the creek nearby. We would see her strutting and scratching around in the snow, often in the company of the wild birds from the feeder, who seemed to accept her. I wrote to friends about her and took photos of her to back up my claims.

One December day, we came home from running errands to find her laid out on the ground, dead; neck stretched out straight, toes pointed back, regal in death. We found no marks on her of any kind. She had just "up and died" as the say around these parts. We did give her a decent burial.

Reluctantly, we admitted it was for the best. And, I had photos of her, didn't I? But as it so happened, there was no film in the camera, so there were no "Hen-Rietta"-chicken-in-residence photos! But how could we ever forget this special hen who strutted like a queen and soared like an eagle? And now you know the true story of a stubborn little brown hen we laughingly called "HEN-RIETTA".

Eagle Express

By Karl Gillespie as told to Claire Suminski

I have raised cattle in Macon County, North Carolina my whole adult life and so find myself outdoors quite a bit. It was hay cutting time in our field, just north of Lake Emory Dam. I was driving my tractor in the field, right by the outflow of Watauga Creek into the Little Tennessee, when I thought I saw a bald eagle on a large rock on the edge of the creek. That in itself was not too surprising, as we had eagles nesting in the area.

But bald eagles were declared an endangered species in our country in 1978 and by the early 1980's there were no eagles to be found in North Carolina. Since that time bald eagles had been, at first slowly, and then steadily re-populating our state. Now there was a pair of eagles that had nested successfully near the Lake Emory Dam for the past two years.

As I got closer to the eagle, it was clear that the noise of the engine and closeness of the tractor that I was riding were getting his attention. It looked like he was trying to fly away, but I could not tell what was preventing him.

Then something amazing happened. He flapped his big, powerful wings two or three times and then rose straight up into the air like a helicopter! As he rose, I could see that he was carrying a very large fish. The pieces of the puzzle were coming together in my mind. The eagle had worked hard to land that fish, to feed himself and probably the eaglets in the nest nearby. Instinct told him to leave, but he was not about to abandon his family's dinner! That day I witnessed a once in a lifetime experience, right from the seat of my tractor, as that majestic bird rose straight up into the sky, like a helicopter, his catch firmly grasped in his talons.

It was truly a sight to behold!

The Annual Pooch Plunge

By Pat Menninger

Most kids love to go to the community pool on hot summer days and to meet their friends and cool off. How many dogs must long to jump in the water, too?! It's against the rules at most pools, but the Recreational Park in Pat's hometown sets aside the last day of the summer for dogs only. No kids allowed! This story is told from the point of view of Pat's dog!

Summer is almost over. I can tell because I hear the honking of the geese as they fly overhead on their way to warmer places. And the wind is blowing cooler.

I always love a car ride, but I can tell this is no ordinary trip to the park. Suddenly, I realize we're at the city pool for the Annual Pooch Plunge! Tomorrow they'll drain the water from the pool. Today the dogs get the last swim of the season.

Yelping with joy, I drag "Mom" across the parking lot to join the pack of dogs waiting impatiently for the gate to open. With tails wagging, we greet friends, old and new, and eagerly wait for the fun to start. Hundreds of yellow balls bob in the sparkling water as we jostle for a spot in the party. It's chaos, a glorious uproar. People are laughing. Dogs are barking. It's almost as much fun as the park.

Today:
Dogs Only!
NO KIDS ALLOWED.

Flossie The Wonder Horse
The Birthday Party

by Kathy Kuhlman

Flossie was invited to my birthday parties, as she would provide pony rides for all the kids in attendance. Kids would take turns riding Flossie around the farm yard. Those who had never ridden before, would receive directions as to how to put their foot into the stirrup, grab the horn and pull themselves up into the saddle. They learned to hold the reins, how to turn right or left, and MOST IMPORTANT OF ALL, how to stop. They were instructed to put only the ball and toes of their feet into the stirrup and not the whole foot. This was important because if they were ever to fall off, it would keep them from getting their foot caught in the stirrup and being dragged. They were then led around until they felt confident enough to ride by themselves.

While the party-goers were waiting for their turn to ride Flossie, they played tag, hide-and-go-seek, and Ante-I-Over (in this game a ball is thrown over the roof of a building to an opposing team. If they catch it, they'll sneak around the building to tag team members that originally threw the ball).

Sometimes, for a gathering of kids, I would hitch Flossie up to my red wagon with a harness that my Dad and I had rigged up for her. I would ride on Flossie's back to steer her using a bridle, as she pulled the wagon behind with kids giggling joyfully. Sometimes my dog, Mickey, would even get into the wagon for a ride.

The party continued with a picnic: Kool-Aid, barbecue, and potato salad. Dessert was an angel food cake with white icing, served with vanilla ice cream. Flossie was rewarded for making the party a great success by receiving a piece of cake. Yes, Flossie had a sweet tooth and she particularly enjoyed angel food cake, which was my favorite too!

More Than A Number

by Melinda as told to Claire Suminski

I first saw this beautiful blue and gold Macaw at our local pet store. His owner had not been able to keep him so he ended up at the Pet Store. Macaws are birds that can talk. I had an older house mate who was home bound and I thought that a bird might be a good companion for her. This South American parrot seemed quite interesting, so I asked the owner for some details.

He said that this bird's name was "Seven" because he was born in Franklin,NC, the 7th day of the 7th month of 2007 and that I could have him for $1,500. Seven had one little problem. He had learned some very bad language from his previous owner. I was up for the challenge, but unfortunately, $1500 was way more than my budget, so I said my goodbyes and left. That evening the owner called me and asked if I would still like to take Seven home for a reduced amount of $500. He said that a kindergarten class had come in as part of a field trip. As they walked in the door, Seven squawked some rude profanities that did not go over well! The pet store owner decided he had better find a new home for Seven and quick! I said yes and this started a new chapter in my life. In captivity, Macaws are known to live over 60 years! This was going to be a serious commitment.

When Seven first joined our family, he swore all the time! He was trying to get our attention, but we decided that when he swore we would ignore him. When he spoke nicely, we would give him lots of attention. This was a good strategy and soon, the bad language faded away. I knew parrots spoke words, but I did not know how much went on in their minds. I could see that this bird was smart. As he spoke more words around us, his communication skills impressed me. He would tease our dogs and play "tug of war" with them with their toys. Also if our dog, Ozzie, tried to go in my bedroom to sleep, Seven would yell, "Ozzie, come back in here", until Ozzie would return to the living room. Seven would then avert his eyes and look at the ceiling, like he did not know who was doing the calling. What a sense of humor!

Seven can work the latch on his cage and let himself in and out, but he does not fly and has no desire to go outside. Every night when he's ready for bed, he will go in his cage and close the latch on the door.

First thing in the morning, he is awake and ready for action. I have to turn on the television if we are to enjoy any peace and quiet in the house! He can watch TV for hours! Macaws are over 13 inches tall and normally their personalities are as bright as their colors. Seven has no problem making himself known! He likes to eat fruits and vegetables and nuts and seeds. But he also likes to eat biscuits! That seems unusual for a parrot. Seven does not fly. He hops and climbs up and down. One laundry day, Seven thought he might help out and got in between the folds of a damp sheet. He ended up in the dryer! Squawks of "Help, HELP!!!" came from inside the dryer, as it spun around, but he was soon released. He was a little fluffier, but none the worse for wear.

My roommate does love Seven and they are true companions. In time, I married a wonderful man; a Walmart manager. Seven calls me "Mama", and everyday when I leave for work at a local beauty salon, Seven squawks, "Goodbye Mama, have a good time at WALMARTTTTT!" This is his humor, shining through again. As our dog, Ozzie, got older, his health started to decline. One day we knew it was time to take Ozzie to the vet and have him put to sleep. We came back to the house that day without Ozzie. It was a sad time for our household and I was not sure how much Seven really understood what was happening. Not long after that, our housemate had a medical incident and had to leave by ambulance. As the first responders wheeled her out on the gurney, I heard Seven urgently scream, "No, Mama, Nooooo!!!!!!" It tugged at my heart. Seven was afraid our housemate might not come back. She soon returned home and Seven was content again. Seven has brought a lot of humor and joy to our lives.

Seven is definitely more than a number!

Cubs Galore!

by Christine Ketter

Black bear cubs look so cute and cuddly, it makes you want to hug them. DON'T TRY IT ! ! ! They have large sharp teeth and claws. A very protective Mama bear is much bigger and is always close by, even if you can't see her. Humans should always keep a good distance away from bears and other wild animals.

Black bears eat things like berries, acorns, nuts, corn, seeds, wheat, soybeans, roots, grasses, honey, insects, grubs, fish, frogs and small mammals. Their diet is about 85% vegetation. They must eat a lot because they can grow to over 400 pounds!

We live in the southern-most part of the Blue Ridge Mountains of South Carolina, partly along the South Saluda River, next to 10,000 acres of watershed property. This is restricted wilderness land owned by the City of Greenville, since the 1930's, which supplies clean drinking water to local communities. It is the perfect habitat for black bears having many safe places to rest, plenty of fresh water, wild berries, nuts and lots of other yummy bear food.

Black bears are normally very shy, and non-aggressive. But they are also naturally inquisitive and playful, often venturing onto our property to check things out. We are very fortunate to be able to watch bears and other wildlife safely from inside our log home.

Adult female bears usually give birth to two or three cubs every two years. One spring day, we saw Mama bear very cautiously enter our back yard. Then, much to our surprise, we saw one... two... three... four..... FIVE tiny cubs follow her ! ! ! A litter of cubs of that size is quite rare. She must have been a very healthy, special bear.

The cubs romped and frolicked in our yard for over half an hour. We watched with joy as they playfully wrestled and chased each other. Stretching up onto it's hind feet, one cub tried tirelessly to hoist itself up and into our bird bath to cool off, even though there was a river just a short way down the mountainside. Another cub climbed up a tiny pine tree. When it got near the top, the cub's weight caused the tree trunk to bend toward the ground and break. This little one was quite startled as it fell to the ground with a thump! But soon it was wrestling again with its siblings in the grass. Mama kept a careful watch over her cubs, sitting with her back against a tree, occasionally uttering little grunts and growls to keep them in line.

The cubs will stay with Mama for about one more year. By that time, she will have taught them all they need to know to live in the wilderness. Then Mama will shoo them off to find their own territory, and she will prepare to have more cubs. I can hardly wait to see how many baby bears she will have next. They are so much fun to watch!

Strange Kitty and the Grain Silo Rescue

From Anne Kelleher Gallup as told to Claire Suminski

Martin and Anne married in 1958 and bought an old farmhouse near the town of Hartford, close to the Vermont border, in upstate New York. Dairy farm country. The rolling fields around them went for miles in every direction and in the winter, everything would be covered with a quiet blanket of snow. Martin drove about half an hour every weekday to Sandy Hill Iron and Brass Works on the Hudson River, and then back again in the evening, while Anne taught Home Economics at the High School in nearby Fort Anne.

While Anne was fixing their dinner, Martin would feed their horse and mule. One evening he saw an unusual sight. "Strange Kitty", the grey barn cat, was climbing up the ladder on the outside of the grain silo. He did not know that cats could climb ladders! He placed his ear against the outside of the silo and heard mewing inside. Strange Kitty must have given birth to a litter of kittens inside the old silo. That would explain the mama cat's determination to climb the ladder. Cold weather was coming. How would the kittens survive?

He opened the little door towards the bottom of the silo and peered inside. As his eyes adjusted to the dimly lit interior, he saw two little black kittens huddled together, with their Mama watching from the top of the ladder. He picked up the mewing kittens and placed them in the crook of his arm and headed for the farmhouse. Wouldn't his wife be surprised! The mama cat seemed somehow relieved that she was receiving help. Through the kitchen window, Anne could see Martin coming. She quickly dried her hands on a towel and headed for the back door to meet him. What was he carrying? Two kittens! And so sweet! One was mostly black with a little white spot on her chest. The other was black too, but with big white splotches. They decided to call them Blacky and Marshmallow.

Anne would heat up milk to give them three times daily. She would hold them and pet them and get them used to being with humans. Once Strange Kitty, the mama cat, saw that her little ones were being cared for, she went back to the very important business of keeping the barn free of mice and rats.

As the kittens grew, they took two different paths. Marshmallow went off to join his mother and help out in the barn, but Blackie stayed mostly indoors. She would curl up on Anne's lap at night and purr contentedly. Martin and Anne had two little girls, while living on the farm and as the oldest was approaching school age, they decided to move to the town of Hudson Falls. Anne packed up Blackie in a hamper and brought her to their new home. Strange Kitty and Marshmallow stayed at the farm to help the new owners. Two more moves upgrading to larger housing, two more children and several years later, Blackie was still the beloved family cat. How glad they all were, that Martin rescued the two mewing kittens from the grain silo that day. Especially Anne.

From Zero to Hero

By Carean Kaso

When Rachel decided to adopt a dog, she went to the shelter and asked to see the dog whose time was up. Out came a big fluffy black dog. His fur was matted. He had a big body and small feet that didn't look like they could support his weight. His nose was crooked. He didn't look especially happy to see her. He made no overture of friendship. "What's his name?" Rachel asked. "Zero," they told her. "I'll take him," she said.

Zero had difficulty adjusting to his new home. He wasn't housetrained. He growled at her friends. He stole food off the kitchen counter. If it came in a bag, he ate the bag too. But Rachel was patient. She bathed him and brushed out his coat. She thought he looked like a bear. He was fun to hug. They had both been lonely, but now they had each other. She talked to him for hours, and they grew close.

One night, Rachel awoke to a frightening sound. Zero was growling low, and deep in his throat. The sound came from the door to her studio apartment. Someone was trying to get in. As she watched, the door knob turned slowly back and forth. Zero's growl rose in his throat. "I'm going to sic my dog on you!" she yelled. There was a commotion on the other side of the door. In one fluid motion, Rachel wrenched open the door and Zero catapulted through it. In the streetlight, Rachel watched as Zero grabbed the man's pant leg as he vaulted the fence. The man cried out, shook his leg free, and got away.

After the police left, Rachel held Zero for a long time, pressing her face into his soft fur. She thought about what might have happened if her friend hadn't been there to protect her. Then the thought hit her like a lightning bolt, and she said "Hero! From now on, you're my Hero!"

And this is how Zero became a Hero!

The Silver Haired Lady and the Baby Possum Rescue

By Sharon Archer of Appalachian Animal Rescue

This story is written from the point of view of one of the baby possums.

Lost and on the side of a road in the wee hours of the morning, my four brothers, five sisters and I were all huddled together when a kind police officer stopped and picked us up. She placed all of us in a box with a very warm and soft blanket. Oh, it was wonderful to get warm!

The police officer was talking to someone as we started moving. She told us not to be afraid, but that she was taking all of us to a silver haired lady who loves possums and tries to help all kinds of wildlife. The ride was strange. We were moving, yet we were still all together in the box when we stopped. A different voice was speaking with the police officer, when all of a sudden someone picked up the box and was speaking softly to us. "All right my little ones, let's get you inside and see what's going on."

My brothers, sisters and I stayed as close to each other as we could, but one by one the silver haired lady checked us over. She weighed us, looked for any injuries and then she gave us a bath and made sure we were warm. One by one she told us that she would need to be able tell us apart. She gave each one of us a special jewel-toned dot on the top of each of our heads. We looked regal! For three to four weeks, the silver haired lady fed us with warm goat's milk, fruit, yogurt and other treats that helped us grow strong. Our bedding was clean, warm and soft.

One day, the silver haired lady said, "The time has come that you must start living in another area outside, where you will be protected." The ground felt different, but there was so much more room! Sleeping during the day is what we possums do, but look out for the night time! We had new food that we ate , the trees and ropes we climbed on were BIG. And the smells and the sounds that we hadn't heard since the police officer found us were a little scary.

Time passed, we were all growing very quickly and eating so much food that our home was getting too small for the ten of us to be together. So the silver haired lady opened the gate so we could explore outside our home. "As long as you stay on the lodge property you can wander and meet other possums and other critters. I will leave the gate to your yard unlocked, and continue to feed you until you want to leave and make your own home."

Exploring we did go. The darkness of the night was awesome! Our eyesight is better in the dark. All of my brothers and sisters returned night after night to our home that the silver haired lady provided for us.

Then one by one we made new friends and made our own homes on the lodge property. We still visit the silver haired lady at night, however she is usually sleeping!

Shhhh!

The Virginia opossum is North America's only marsupial (a mammal that carries its young in a pouch). Possums eat ticks, slugs, cockroaches, carcasses and even snakes. Things that humans think are gross, are eaten regularly by possums. They help to keep nature balanced and are native to the southern United States.

The Brave Little Screech—Owls of Brush Creek

By Martha Lind

One evening at dusk, Mom, Dad and I were sitting on the front porch of our old home place on Brush Creek, in Swain County, deep in the mountains of Western North Carolina. Dad tended our property after retiring from many years of working with roofing and sheet metal in Lakeland, Florida and my mother and I were both nurses. We surely did enjoy our mountain home.

There was a young Pecan tree beside the front porch. It was the perfect place for three young Screech Owls whose mother had brought them off the nest for their first flight. They still had that baby bird look with downy feathers. As they sat, they communicated back and forth with a soft breathy whooshing sound. We were mesmerized by their beauty and bravery, as they took short test flights to the black walnut tree below the garden, then back. Whoosh... Whoosh...Whoosh

They knew we were there and one of them screwed up the courage to come sit on the porch railing to get a better look at us. I suppose we must have looked odd to them, but they did not show fright, just an almost friendly curiosity. It was probably similar to the looks on our faces as we watched them with awe.

After all these years, I still cherish the shared experience I had with my folks that evening on our front porch. Sometimes we are given these gifts. They bring sweet peace into our hearts and remembering them brings back that amazing wonder and grace.

The Skunk Convoy

By Cliff as told to Claire Suminski

Cliff and his wife, Mavis, live in the suburbs of Columbus, Ohio. Like many Northerners, on hot summer nights they enjoy opening their bedroom window to enjoy some cool, fresh air. All was well and good until a family of skunks took up residence in their back yard. They would open a window, but before long, one of the skunks would let loose with that infamous skunk scent. Cliff would mutter under his breath, and shut the window. Another stuffy night!

All of the backyards in Mavis and Cliff's neighborhood were connected, with no fences. It was as if there was one large common backyard that ran the length of their street. A fox hound and a Heinz 57 mutt, known as "The Mottly Mutleys", lived in the house next door. These dogs had chased after the skunks one night with disastrous results. Their skunk encounter ended in a tomato juice bath and two days of confinement in the garage. Now they were gun shy. One night the dogs went out in the back yard to relieve themselves before bed and the fox hound heard something. Following his powerful nose, he headed towards Cliff's yard and there encountered an adorable baby skunk. That baby skunk was scared and instinctively turned around to let the invading dog have it. But the foxhound, probably remembering his past skunk experience, high tailed it out of there before the baby skunk could spray. Cliff and Mavis had quite an interesting show out of their bedroom window that night!

One evening soon after that, Cliff looked out his window and saw 7 skunks lined up shoulder to shoulder, along the back edge of his yard, heading towards his house. They looked like a side by side truck convoy! As the skunks came closer , his nose twitched at their very particular skunk scent . He turned to his wife and said," Mavis, they smell like burnt coffee!"

Cliff and Mavis later discovered that their neighbors to the North were leaving bowls of cat food out all the time in their back yard to feed their kitty. Unbeknownst to them, they had also been feeding a growing skunk population!

When Cliff had knee surgery that August, the doctor urged him to take walks around the block as soon as he was able. During an evening stroll, as he turned the corner and was heading back towards his house, a skunk started following him down the sidewalk. He leaned on his cane a little more and picked up the pace. The skunk matched his speed. Soon Cliff was going as fast as he could and really getting a workout. When he reached the front porch, Mavis opened the screen door and yelled, "Cliff, why are you all sweaty? Are you all right?" He replied, "Mavis, it's that skunk. He's chasing me! But when Cliff turned to point at the skunk, it had disappeared into the bushes. However, there was no denying that telltale burnt coffee scent that hung in the air.

As they got ready for bed that night, Cliff said to his wife in a sheepish voice. "Mavis, let's not open the window tonight, I guess air conditioning is not so bad after all!"

20 And God said, Let the waters bring forth abundantly the moving creature that hath life, and fowl [that] may fly above the earth in the open firmament of heaven.

21 And God created great whales, and every living creature that moveth, which the waters brought forth abundantly, after their kind, and every winged fowl after his kind: and God saw that [it was] good.

22 And God blessed them, saying, Be fruitful, and multiply, and fill the waters in the seas, and let fowl multiply in the earth.

23 And the evening and the morning were the fifth day.

24 And God said, Let the earth bring forth the living creature after his kind, cattle, and creeping thing, and beast of the earth after his kind: and it was so.

25 And God made the beast of the earth after his kind, and cattle after their kind, and every thing that creepeth upon the earth after his kind: and God saw that [it was] good.

Genesis 1:20-25 KJV

...and GOD saw that it was good.

The Buck Stops Here

Several individuals have contributed to the writing and illustrating of this book. These two women have taken the lead in gathering, compiling and revising these contributions so that they fit together as a whole.

Meet Lead Author and Storyteller: Claire Suminski

Claire enjoys collecting stories from family members, friends and from her travels. She often remarks that God made all of the different animals, not man, and what what an amazing job He did! Claire was raised in the Adirondack region of New York. She and her husband, Joe, moved to Western North Carolina in 1991. The Suminski Family enjoys their small working farm, which is nestled in a peaceful mountain valley along the Little Tennessee River. Writing stories that awaken wonder in the hearts of children, brings her great joy.

Meet Lead Illustrator and Graphic Designer: Susan Swedlund

Susan is a multi-media artist. She works as a graphic artist for Suminski Family Books, does open air water color painting and works with clay. She loves making ceramic pieces and teaching others the fundamentals of working with clay. While Susan and her husband reside in Beloit, Wisconsin, they enjoy spending a portion of the year in Franklin, North Carolina. Susan's illustrative work can be seen on pages 0,2,4,6, 10-13, 17, 23-25 and the front and back cover.

Authors

Christine Ketter: *Cubs Galore!*
Christine grew up in a mountainous area of Northern New Jersey. Whether swimming or canoeing the lakes and rivers, hiking a tree covered mountain, or simply sitting in the woods looking for critters, she always felt most at home surrounded by wilderness. Christine and her husband Ken live in a log home in the South Carolina Upstate where they enjoy hiking, kayaking and birding. Currently working in downtown Greenville, Christine finds the long commute well worth it, as coming home always seems like being on a mini vacation.

Karl Gillespie: *Eagle Express*
Karl has served as a Macon County Commissioner since 2016. He is a fifth generation Marconian and is married to Macon County native, Janet Taylor Gillespie. They raise registered black Angus cattle on their family farm. They are grateful to have their son, Logan, working with them, bringing another generation of ideas and knowledge to their family's pursuits. Karl is currently running for NC House of Representatives and is proud to be from Western North Carolina.

Kathy Kuhlman: *The Birthday Party: Flossie the Wonder Horse*
Kathy, a farm girl from North Dakota, was a high school teacher, college Associate Professor, and county 4-H agent. She currently lives in Western North Carolina with her husband, Lou. They designed and physically built their home, located in the mountains. She replaced her real horses with saw horses which proved to be more practical in their building project, and didn't require expensive feed nor veterinary care! Kathy is currently enjoying retirement.

Mike Kurczewski: *The Hungry Sea Lion*
Mike is a retired Ohio State Trooper who has been part of the diving industry for over 35 years. He and his wife, Kelli, now reside in the mountains of Western North Carolina, in Macon County. Mike has done public safety police diving, evidence recovery and trained diving instructors through PADI. He has had diving encounters with turtles, sharks, eels, sea horses, tiger seals and more.

Authors

Anne Kelleher Gallup: *Strange Kitty and the Grain Silo Rescue*

Anne was raised in Fort Edward, New York, a small mill town on the Hudson River. She graduated from Syracuse University and became a Home Economics Teacher. She has always loved music, art and books. Anne and her cat, Blackie, were steadfast companions through the years. She now resides in the Good Shepherd Home, near the Adirondack Park, in upstate New York.

Sharon Archer: *The Silver Haired Lady and the Baby Possum Rescue*

Sharon is proud to have been raised in Baltimore, Maryland. She and her husband of 35 years enjoy living in Franklin, NC. Sharon retired from Western Carolina University and has been a volunteer with NC Wildlife Rehabilitation for 25 years. She has been a very important part of the development of Appalachian Animal Rescue. And she has a special fondness for possums!

Martha Lind: *The Brave Little Screech Owls of Brush Creek*

Martha was raised in Lakeland, Florida. Her Mother was very proud to be the first person in the family to graduate from college with a nursing degree. Martha and her two sisters followed in their mother's footsteps and became nurses as well. Martha attended the Rabun Gap Nacoochee School and was part of the Fox Fire Staff. She has always enjoyed collecting and sharing stories. She currently resides at Grandview Care Center.

Authors & Illustrators

Marilyn Miller:
Marilyn wrote and Illustrated *'The Short Stubborn Life of Hen-Reitta"* (pg.2-4) and illustrated *"The Brave Little Screech Owls of Brush Creek"* (pg.23). She works primarily in acrylics and continues to perfect her technique. Her paintings often reflect her love for the local area. She joined Macon County Art Association in 1992 and has received many community awards celebrating her art. Marilyn is a happy resident of The Franklin House and blesses many with her art.

Pat Menninger:
Pat wrote and illustrated *"The Pooch Plunge"* (pg.8), and illustrated *"The Baby Possum Rescue"* (pg.20,22) and *"The Skunk Convoy"* (pg.24-26). She believes that art should be uplifting. She strives to make each piece a positive experience for herself and those around her. Pat enjoys playing her flute and exploring all art mediums. She wrote and illustrated "The Adventures of Silly Tilly" and illustrated "Pricilla Pig's Culinary Crisis". Her art can be seen at The Uptown Gallery in Franklin, NC where she lives with her husband and their much loved Pomeranian, Sweetie.

Carean Kasco:
Carean is a writer and illustrator and she wrote and illustrated *"From Zero to Hero"* (pgs. 18,19). She also serves as volunteer coordinator at the Appalachian Animal Rescue Center. Carean lives with her husband and five rescue dogs in the mountains of North Carolina.

Illustrators

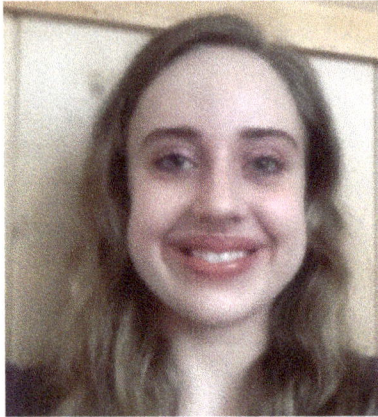

Sydney Giaquinto:
Sydney is a sophomore at Western Carolina University with an emphasis in film and creative writing. She is a fan of old movies and antiques. Sydney loves life and hopes to bring positive change to the world around her. She illustrated the story "More Than a Number".

Annie Suminski:
Annie is a graduate of the University of South Florida. She does bookkeeping by day and likes to weave, crochet, Contra dance, sing ballads, and read books by night. Her Angora goats are on permanent vacation at the Cowee Mountain Valley Farm. The mountain graphic design, seen throughout this book, was originally a silkscreen print done by Annie.

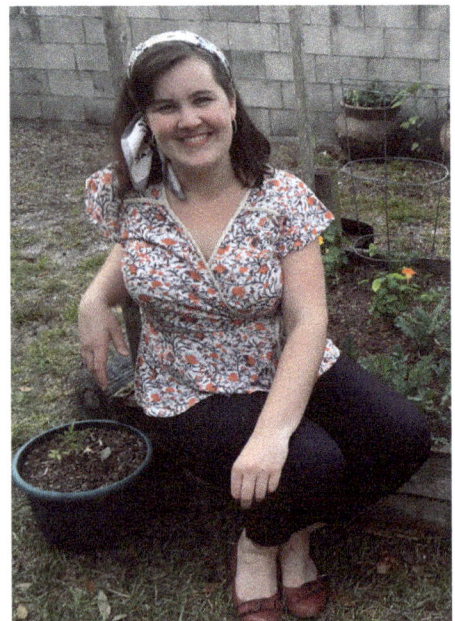

Animal Names

Circle the words from the list below. You will find the words going across and up & down.

```
T M Y L K E A G L E K R C V T
N P D L P O N Y W O B M R A R
S H V S G B S S B P M X P S F
V E B V O F Y M U S K U N K S
B N M E V L O B S T E R W L P
N D P O O C H P B V I B I V D
R K Q O C T O P U S S P K T O
A O A Y H H C T F F E E M W G
D O N K E Y B L X B A X O S B
V B Y B F I S H W Y L O Z H O
B Q U E K U N P P U I M C A B
M O W L T A I I I S O A U R C
M H P O S S U M W W N C B K A
S Q U I R R E L T C D A S U T
A H B C X T B E A R W W L K I
```

SQUIRREL	OCTOPUS	LOBSTER	SEA LION
SKUNKS	DONKEY	POSSUM	BOBCAT
POOCH	MACAW	SHARK	EAGLE
PONY	FISH	OWL	BEAR
HEN	DOG	CUBS	

Bonus challenge: There are 5 animals in the list above that were not mentioned in this book. Draw a star next to those five animal names.

The answers can be found in the back of this book.

Animal Actions

Find and crcle the words from the list below. You will find the words going across, up & down and diagonal.

```
T R O T L C T S M S A H Z O B
S W I N G L S S O A R H U Y H
Q T U P V A C S O D Q I G V Z
M Q H D S W R Q W P Y A M R T
Q A H D U J E U Y O K Y J H I
S P N H C W E A F R O L I C L
C L B E J M C W N M W P O H C
A U O W U X H K E S A X N O R
M N U U X V A H G C D Q L P A
P G N C P J E R K A D G T K W
E E D N P I P R Y V L C V N L
R T X D J R U N Z E E L J M F
R R O M P W G V X N T M U N Y
W L J U M P W V J G V N T P Q
Q D O C W Z Y M N E T P H G I
```

SCAVENGE	MANEUVER	SCAMPER	SCREECH
WADDLE	SQUAWK	PLUNGE	GALLUP
CRAWL	FROLIC	SWING	SWOOP
JUMP	ROMP	TROT	RUN
SOAR	CLAW	BOUND	HOP

The answers can be found in the back of this book.

Animal Stories 2 Scramble

Unscramble the words below. There are clues to each scramble written below to help you if needed.

1 nneregddea   _____

2 siurmlpaa   _____

3 ldaeds   _____

4 hocop   _____

5 oerh   _____

6 oremmy   _____

7 xeressp   _____

8 anrchb   _____

9 nvees   _____

10 sntce   _____

Clues:

1. Eagles are...
2. Possums are...
3. To ride Flossie you need a...
4. A ----- plunged
5. Zero's new name
6. The Owl story is a ....
7. Eagle's take off
8. Hen-Rietta's perch
9. A name
10. Skunk aroma

The answers can be found in the back of this book.

Answer Key

Animal Names

```
T M Y L K E A G L E K R C V T
N P D L P O N Y W O B M R A R
S H V S G B S S B P M X P S F
V E B V O F Y M U S K U N K S
B N M E V L O B S T E R W L P
N D P O O C H P B V I B I V D
R K Q O C T O P U S S P K T O
A O A Y H H C T F F E E M W G
D O N K E Y B L X B A X O S B
V B Y B F I S H W Y L O Z H O
B Q U E K U N P P U I M C A B
M O W L T A I I I S O A U R C
M H P O S S U M W W N C B K A
S Q U I R R E L T C D A S U T
A H B C X T B E A R W W L K I
```

⭐SQUIRREL   ⭐OCTOPUS   LOBSTER   SEA LION

SKUNKS   ⭐DONKEY   POSSUM   ⭐BOBCAT

POOCH   MACAW   ⭐SHARK   EAGLE

PONY   FISH   OWL   BEAR

HEN   DOG   CUBS

Animal Actions

```
T R O T L C T S M S A H Z O B
S W I N G L S S O A R H U Y H
Q T U P V A C S O D Q I G V Z
M Q H D S W R Q W P Y A M R T
Q A H D U J E U Y O K Y J H I
S P N H C W E A F R O L I C L
C L B E J M C W N M W P O H C
A U O W U X H K E S A X N O R
M N U U X V A H G C D Q L P A
P G N C P J E R K A D G T K W
E E D N P I P R Y V L C V N L
R T X D J R U N Z E E L J M F
R R O M P W G V X N T M U N Y
W L J U M P W V J G V N T P Q
Q D O C W Z Y M N E T P H G I
```

Animal Stories 2 Scramble

nneregddea	endangered
siurmlpaa	marsupial
ldaeds	saddle
hocop	pooch
oerh	hero
oremmy	memory
xeressp	express
anrchb	branch
nvees	seven
sntce	scent

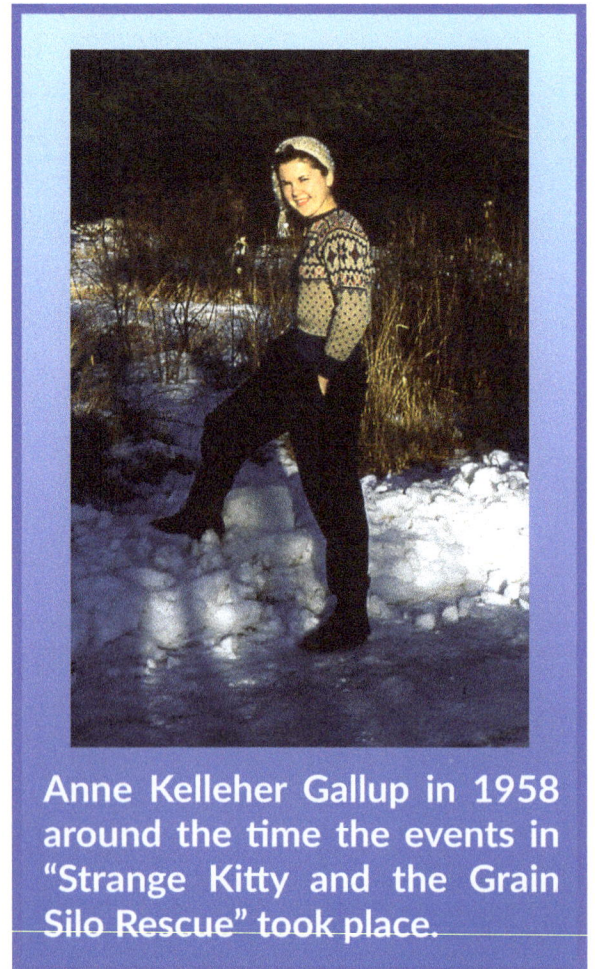

Anne Kelleher Gallup in 1958 around the time the events in "Strange Kitty and the Grain Silo Rescue" took place.

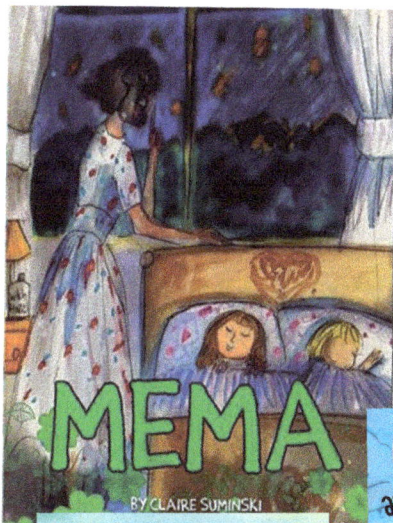

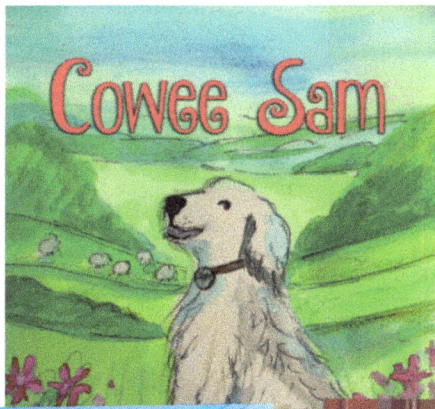

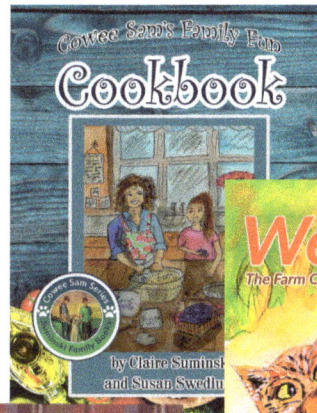

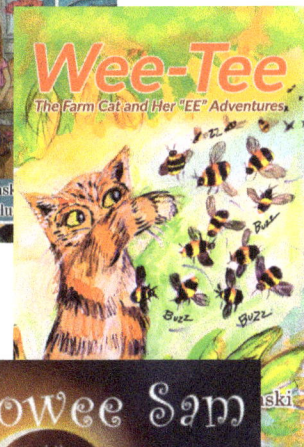

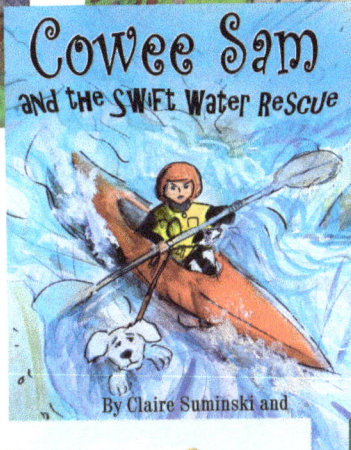

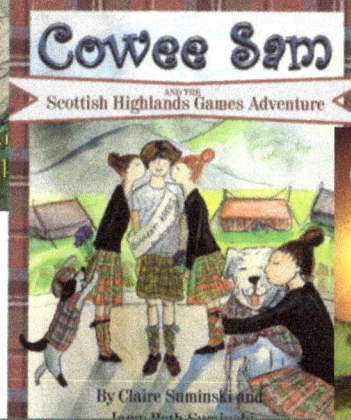

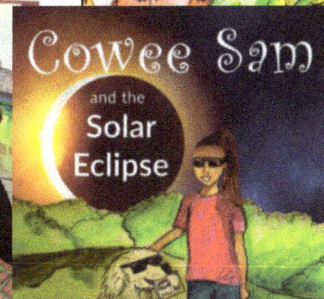

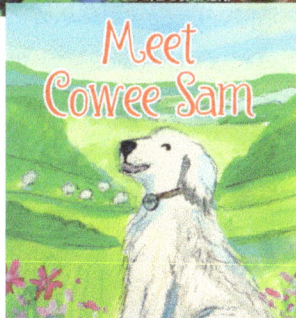

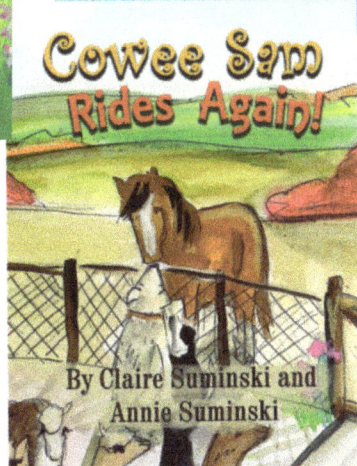

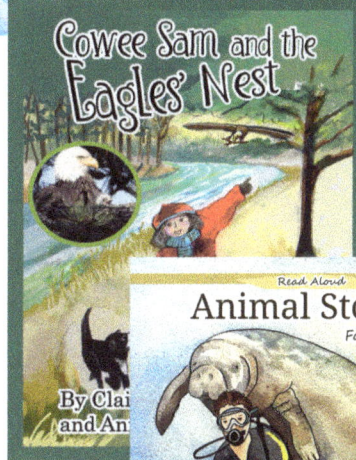

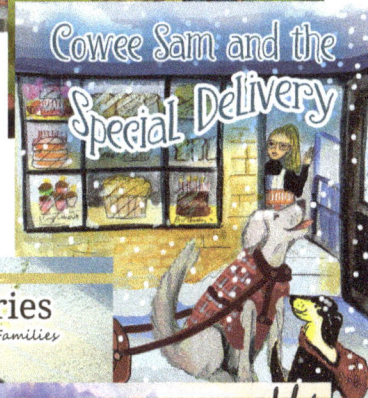

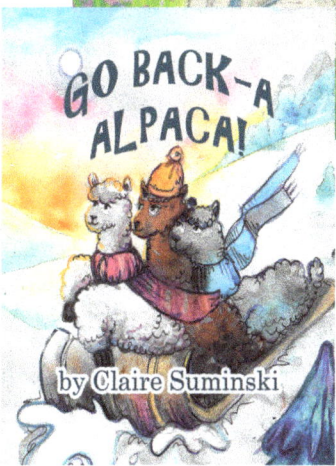

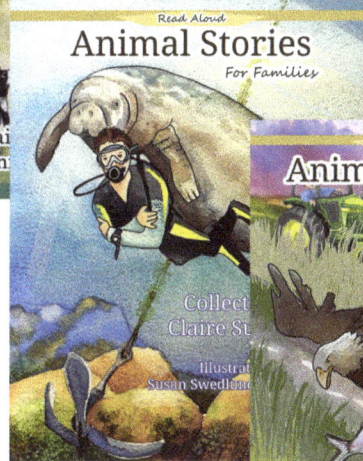

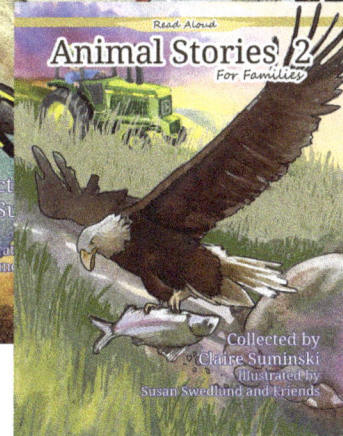

Suminski Family Books Order Form
You may also order on-line at www.suminskifamilybooks.com

Cowee Sam Series $14.95 each

Cowee Sam
Cowee Sam and the Swift Water Rescue
Cowee Sam and the Solar Eclipse
Cowee Sam Rides Again!
Cowee Sam and the Scottish Highlands Games Adventure
Cowee Sam and the Eagles' Nest
Cowee Sam's Family Fun Cookbook
Cowee Sam and the Special Delivery

Reading is an Exciting Adventure Series $8.95 each

Meet Cowee Sam
Wee-Tee the Farm Cat and Her "EE' Adventure

We Survived the Eclipse!
Accounts of the 2017 Total Solar Eclipse in Franklin, NC and Surrounding Areas $19.95

The Early Grade School Reading Series $11.95 each

Go Back-a Alpaca

Read Aloud Animal Stories for Families Series $11.95 each

Animal Stories 1
Animal Stories 2

Please make checks out to **Suminski Family Books**

and send order to : 32 Jim Berry Road Franklin, NC 28734 or email order to: Claire@dometrics.com

Name_____

Address:_____

_____

Phone:_____ Email:_____

Name of Book:	# of Copies	Amount
Free Shipping		
~~Shipping: $2.50 for 1 book/$5.00 2-9 Books/10 or over ships free~~		
(Based on United Postal Service Media Rate)	shipping:	FREE
Total	Total: